CELEBRATING THE CITY OF RHODES

Celebrating the City of Rhodes

Walter the Educator

Silent King Books

Copyright © 2024 by Walter the Educator

All rights reserved. No part of this book may be reproduced in any manner whatsoever without written per- mission except in the case of brief quotations embodied in critical articles and reviews.

First Printing, 2024

Disclaimer

This book is a literary work; the story is not about specific persons, locations, situations, and/or circumstances unless mentioned in a historical context. Any resemblance to real persons, locations, situations, and/or circumstances is coincidental. This book is for entertainment and informational purposes only. The author and publisher offer this information without warranties expressed or implied. No matter the grounds, neither the author nor the publisher will be accountable for any losses, injuries, or other damages caused by the reader's use of this book. The use of this book acknowledges an understanding and acceptance of this disclaimer.

Celebrating the City of Rhodes is a little collectible souvenir book that belongs to the Celebrating Cities Book Series by Walter the Educator. Collect them all and more books at WaltertheEducator.com

USE THE EXTRA SPACE TO TAKE NOTES AND DOCUMENT YOUR MEMORIES

RHODES

In the dawn's embrace, Rhodes awakens bright,

Celebrating the City of Rhodes

An island wrapped in dawn's first light,

Ancient stones whisper tales untold,

Of knights, of kings, of glories bold.

From Lindos' acropolis, high and grand,

To the shores where sapphire waters stand,

The past and present intertwine,

In this realm where histories align.

Echoes of battles, fierce and grand,

Resonate through this storied land,

Where the Colossus once stood tall,

Celebrating the City of
Rhodes

Guardian of the city's call.

Cobblestone streets in Old Town's heart,

Each step a journey, each turn an art,

Medieval walls stand strong and proud,

Embracing whispers from the crowd.

The Palace of the Grand Masters' might,

A fortress of enduring light,

A citadel of strength and grace,

A testament to time's embrace.

The windmill's silent, standing still,

By Mandraki Harbor's tranquil spill,

Three pillars reaching to the sky,

Witnesses to years gone by.

Bazaars bustling with vibrant life,

Hues and fragrances, free from strife,

Celebrating the City of Rhodes

Where traders' voices rise and blend,

In a chorus that will never end.

Aegean waves kiss golden sands,

Caressed by gentle, tender hands,

Where sun-kissed travelers seek repose,

In Rhodes, where the spirit flows.

Mountains rise and valleys deep,

Secrets in their shadows keep,

Olive groves and citrus scent,

A natural world, magnificently bent.

Celebrating the City of
Rhodes

Butterflies in Petaloudes dance,

In a fluttering, delicate trance,

A sanctuary, nature's art,

A place to heal, a place to start.

Kalithea's springs with waters pure,

Offer solace, offer cure,

Healing hands of nature's gift,

In Rhodes, spirits always lift.

ABOUT THE CREATOR

Walter the Educator is one of the pseudonyms for Walter Anderson. Formally educated in Chemistry, Business, and Education, he is an educator, an author, a diverse entrepreneur, and he is the son of a disabled war veteran. "Walter the Educator" shares his time between educating and creating. He holds interests and owns several creative projects that entertain, enlighten, enhance, and educate, hoping to inspire and motivate you. Follow, find new works, and stay up to date with Walter the Educator™ at WaltertheEducator.com

www.ingramcontent.com/pod-product-compliance
Lightning Source LLC
LaVergne TN
LVHW012048070526
838201LV00082B/3859